DC COMICS™

WONDER WOMAN ORIGAMI

AMAZING FOLDING PROJECTS
FEATURING THE WARRIOR PRINCESS

Published by Capstone Press in 2015
A Capstone Imprint
1710 Roe Crest Drive
North Mankato, Minnesota 56003
www.capstonepub.com

STAR35426

Library of Congress Cataloging-in-Publication Data
Montroll, John, author.
  Wonder Woman origami : amazing folding projects featuring
the warrior princess / by John Montroll ; Wonder Woman created
by William Moulton Marston.
       pages cm.—(DC super heroes. DC origami)
  Summary: "Provides instructions and diagrams for folding
origami models of characters, objects, and symbols related to
Wonder Woman"—Provided by publisher.
  Audience: Age 8–12.
  Audience: Grades 4–6.
  Includes bibliographical references.
  ISBN 978-1-4914-1788-1 (library binding)
  ISBN 978-1-4914-7595-9 (eBook PDF)
1. Origami—Juvenile literature. 2. Wonder Woman (Fictitious
character)—Juvenile literature. 3. Superheroes in art—Juvenile
literature. 4. Handicraft—Juvenile literature. I. Marston,
William Moulton, 1893–1947, creator. II. Title.
  TT872.5.M685 2015
  736.982—dc23   2015003763

EDITORIAL CREDITS

Editor and Model Folder: Christopher Harbo
Designer: Lori Bye
Art Directors: Bob Lentz and Nathan Gassman
Contributing Writers: Donald Lemke and Michael Dahl
Folding Paper Illustrator: Min Sung Ku
Production Specialist: Kathy McColley

PHOTO CREDITS

Capstone Studio/Karon Dubke, all photos

Printed in the United States of America in North Mankato, MN.
052015 008823CGF15

TABLE OF CONTENTS

PAPER PERFECTION 4
SYMBOLS 6   BASIC FOLDS 7

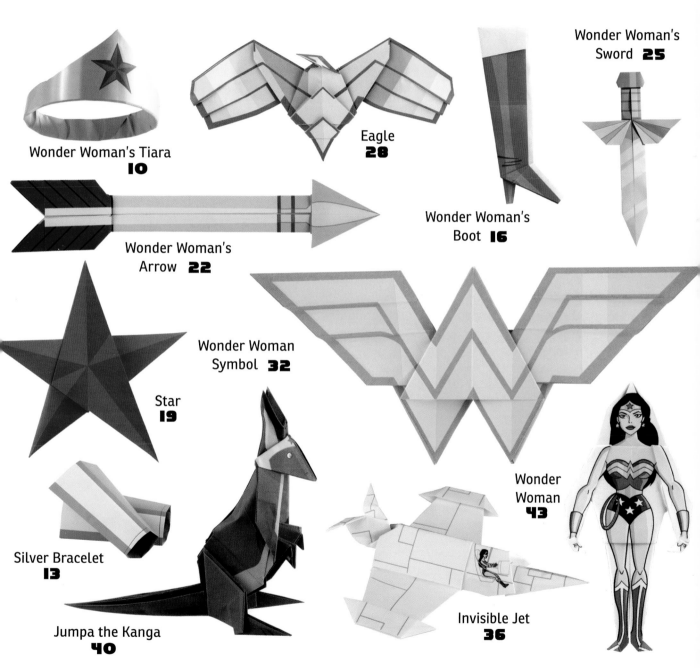

Paper Perfection

Capturing Wonder Woman, as any of her archenemies could tell you, is nearly impossible. Armed with a golden tiara, silver bracelets, a Lasso of Truth, and expert combat skills, she deftly avoids the clutches of evil. But where villains fail, you can succeed—at least when it comes to capturing the spirit of the Amazonian warrior. How? With your powers of paper folding!

Get ready to transform paper into the most remarkable collection of origami objects, symbols, and figures ever created for Wonder Woman. From her silver bracelets and golden tiara to her mighty sword and symbolic eagle, every model you fold is guaranteed to amaze. When you reveal your secret skills, your friends will beg you for paper versions of Jumpa the Kanga and the Invisible Jet.

Whether you have experience with origami or will be folding for the first time, this collection will help you succeed. The folding diagrams are drawn in the internationally approved Randlett-Yoshizawa style. This style is easy to follow once you learn the basic folds outlined in the pages to come. The models are also ranked and organized for their level of difficulty. Simple models have one star, intermediate models have two stars, and the most complex models have three stars.

Just remember, Wonder Woman didn't become a super hero overnight. She trained for years and tested herself against her warrior sisters before joining the fight for truth and justice. To build your folding skills, work through this collection from simplest to most complex. Only through patience and practice will you capture the Princess of the Amazons with paper perfection.

Symbols

Lines

— — — — — — — —   Valley fold, fold in front.

—··—··—··—··—   Mountain fold, fold behind.

———————   Crease line.

··············   X-ray or guide line.

Arrows

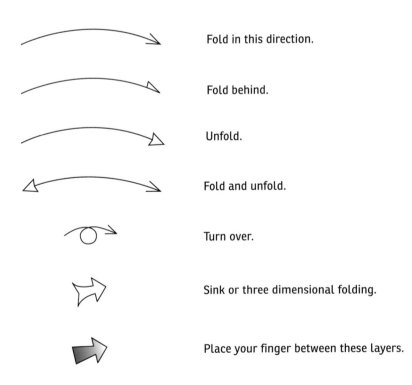

Fold in this direction.

Fold behind.

Unfold.

Fold and unfold.

Turn over.

Sink or three dimensional folding.

Place your finger between these layers.

BASIC FOLDS

PLEAT FOLD

Fold back and forth. Each pleat is composed of one valley and mountain fold. Here are two examples.

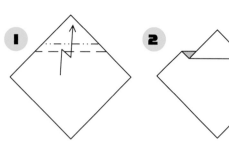

Pleat-fold.

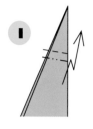

Pleat-fold.

SQUASH FOLD

In a squash fold, some paper is opened and then made flat. The shaded arrow shows where to place your finger.

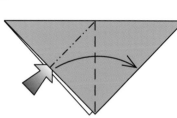
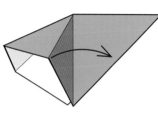
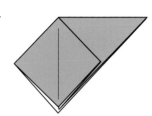

Squash-fold.

A 3D step.

INSIDE REVERSE FOLD

In an inside reverse fold, some paper is folded between layers. The inside reverse fold is generally referred to as a reverse fold. Here are two examples.

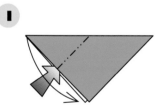

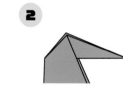

Reverse-fold.

Reverse-fold.

PETAL FOLD

In a petal fold, one point is folded up while two opposite sides meet each other.

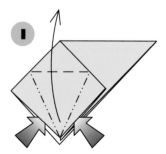
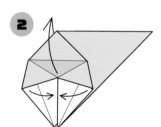
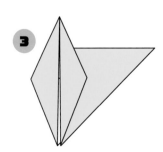

7

CRIMP FOLD

A crimp fold is a combination of two reverse folds. Open the model slightly to form the crimp evenly on each side. Here are two examples.

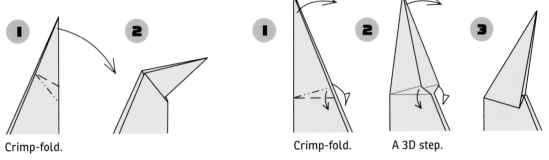

Crimp-fold.   Crimp-fold.   A 3D step.

RABBIT EAR

To fold a rabbit ear, one corner is folded in half and laid down to a side.

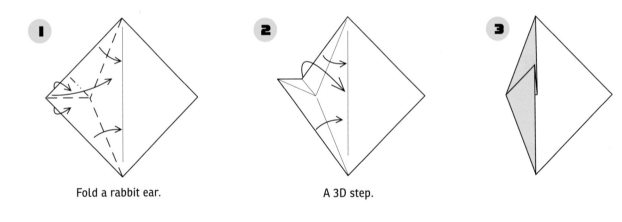

Fold a rabbit ear.   A 3D step.

SINK

For a sink, some of the paper without edges is folded inside. To do this fold, much of the model must be unfolded.

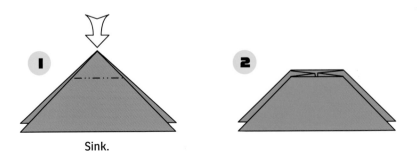

Sink.

PRELIMINARY FOLD

The preliminary fold is the starting point for many models. The maneuver in step 3 occurs in many other models.

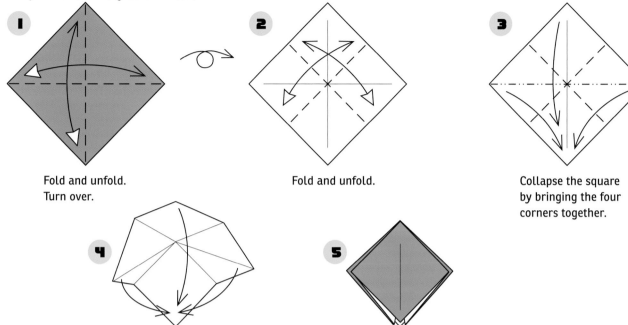

Fold and unfold.
Turn over.

Fold and unfold.

Collapse the square by bringing the four corners together.

This is 3D.

Preliminary Fold

WATERBOMB BASE

The waterbomb base is named for the waterbomb balloon which is made from it.

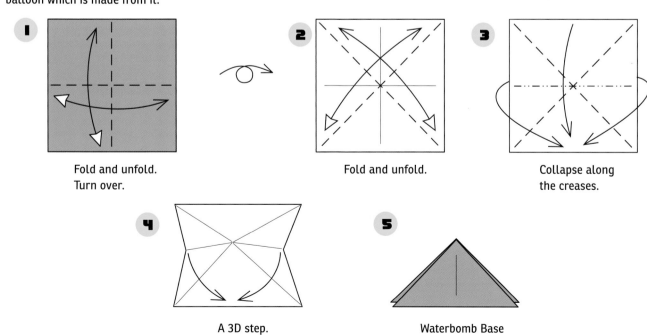

Fold and unfold.
Turn over.

Fold and unfold.

Collapse along the creases.

A 3D step.

Waterbomb Base

WONDER WOMAN'S TIARA

Princess Diana, known to the world as Wonder Woman, is a true sovereign. Her mother, Hippolyta, is Queen of the Amazons, a race of warrior women who inhabit the hidden island of Themyscira. To declare her royal blood, Wonder Woman wears a golden tiara—which also serves as a weapon! With a flick of the wrist, she flings it through the air like a ninja star. The tiara's sharp, almost unbreakable metal can slice through rock, wire, and steel, giving the hero a crowning edge over her foes.

LEVEL: ★☆☆

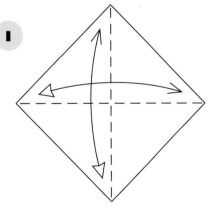

Fold and unfold.

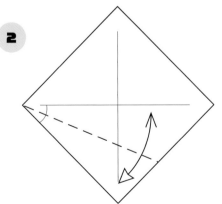

Fold and unfold.

3

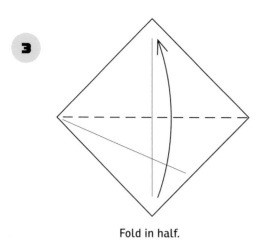

Fold in half.

4

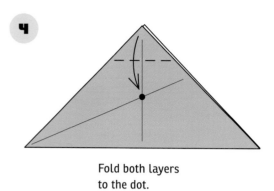

Fold both layers
to the dot.

5

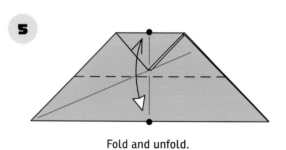

Fold and unfold.

6

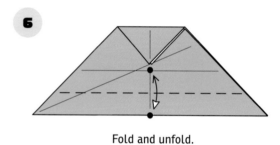

Fold and unfold.

7

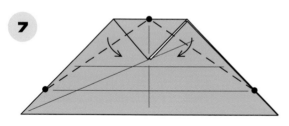

Fold on the left and right.

8

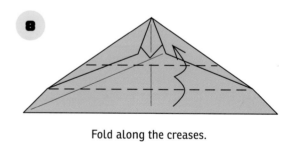

Fold along the creases.

9

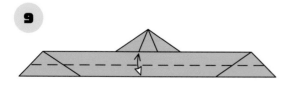

Fold in half and unfold.

10

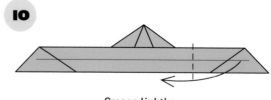

Crease lightly.

11

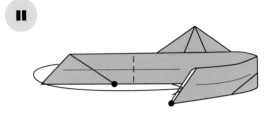

Tuck inside. The
dots will meet.

12

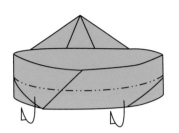

Fold inside and make
the band round.

13

Fold the edges to
shape the tiara.

14

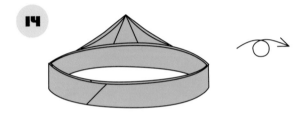

Turn over.

15

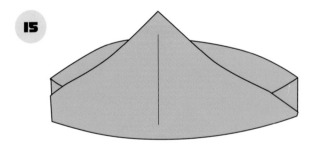

Wonder Woman's Tiara

SILVER BRACELET

Wonder Woman frequently faces foes with fearsome weapons. Yet she wears no armor, and she carries no shield. Her gear is built for speed and freedom of movement, not for protection. But the Amazonian warrior does, it turns out, have a secret defense: her silver bracelets. The jewelry serves her better than a bulletproof vest. Combined with dazzling acrobatics, swiftness, and strength, the bracelets deflect arrows, axes, spears, swords—and even bullets. Trust the Princess of the Amazons to turn a little silver bling into a buffer zone.

LEVEL: ★☆☆

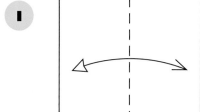

1 Fold and unfold.

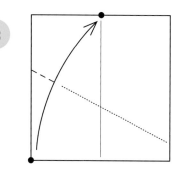

2 Fold up so the dots meet. Crease on the left.

3

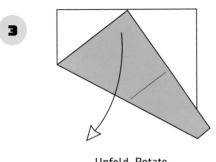

Unfold. Rotate
model 180°.

4

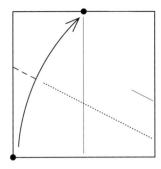

Repeat steps 2–3.

5

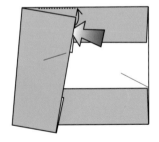

Fold to the dots.

6

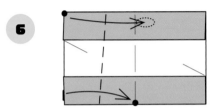

Bring the left edge to the dot
at the bottom and the upper
left corner into the top strip.

7

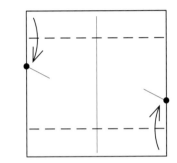

Slide the paper up to the
edge at the dotted line.

8

Tuck inside.

9

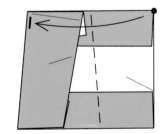

Bring the dot close to the
left edge. Fold at an angle
similar to that in step 6.

10

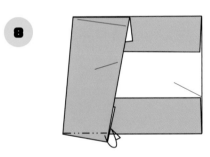

Slide the paper up to the
edge at the dotted line.

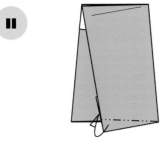

11

Fold behind.

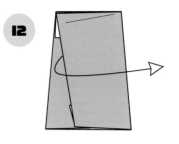

12

Unfold.

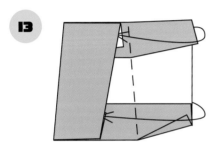

13

The model is 3D on the right. Tuck inside the pockets.

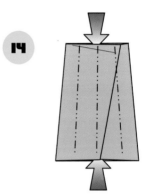

14

Shape the bracelet with soft folds to make it round. Repeat behind.

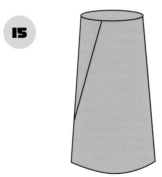

15

Silver Bracelet

WONDER WOMAN'S BOOT

The Princess of the Amazons doesn't stand for mundane footwear. As a warrior she needs the best possible gear. Since she can fly on the slightest of breezes, swim with the strength of a shark, and grapple with gods, normal boots would not be up to the task. Her red and white Amazonian "kicks" give her incredible traction. They also provide her with an aerodynamic advantage as she glides over major cities, endless oceans, or the outskirts of Olympus to confront the agents of chaos and dread.

LEVEL: ★★☆

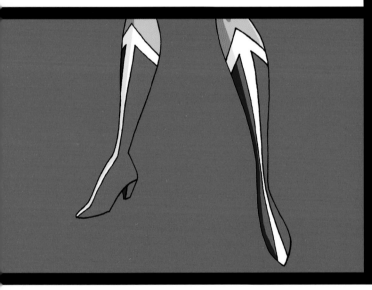

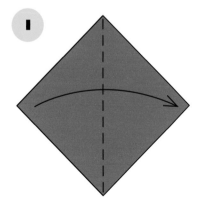
1 Fold in half.

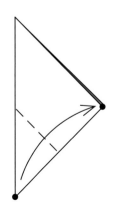
2 The dots will meet.

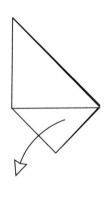
3 Unfold.

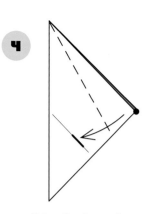

4

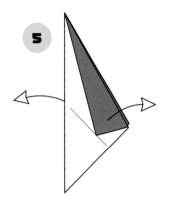

Bring the dot to the
crease, repeat behind.

5

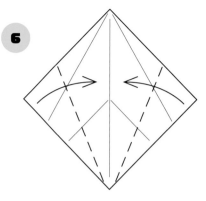

Unfold everything.

6

Fold close to the center.

7

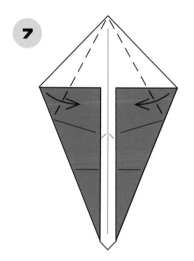

Fold along the creases.

8

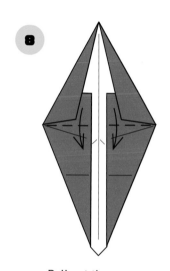

Pull out the corners.

9

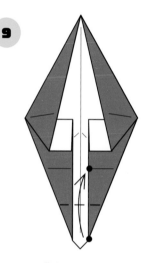

Fold up so the
dots meet.

10

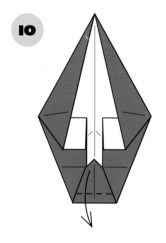

Fold down.

11

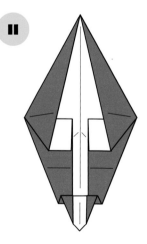

Turn over.

12

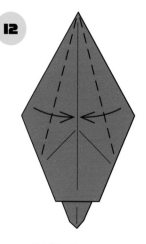

Fold to the center.

13

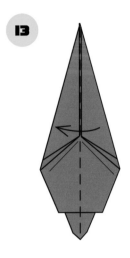

Fold in half.

14

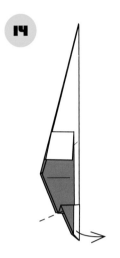

Slide the paper.

15

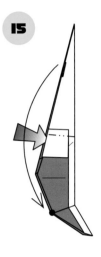

Reverse-fold so the edge meets the dot.

16

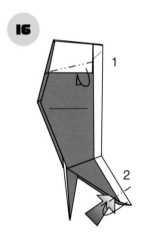

1. Fold inside, repeat behind.
2. Reverse-fold.

17

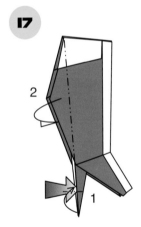

1. Reverse-fold.
2. Wrap around the inner layers, repeat behind.

18

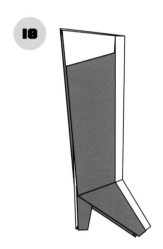

Wonder Woman's Boot

STAR

LEVEL: ★★☆

When Wonder Woman rushes toward bad guys in a ferocious fury of justice, the shining star on her golden tiara is the first thing they see. The red, white, and blue of America, as well as the stars on its flag, inspired Princess Diana to create a uniform suitable for a freedom-loving warrior. The blazing symbol on her crown represents the powers of truth and light. It shines as a beacon of hope in a world threatened by darkness. Among all the crime-fighting champions of peace, Wonder Woman is truly a star.

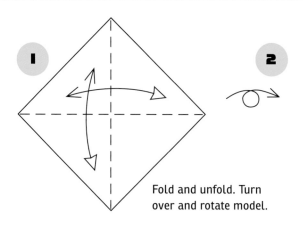

1. Fold and unfold. Turn over and rotate model.

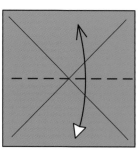

2. Fold and unfold.

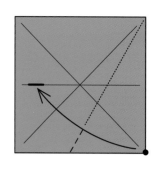

3. Bring the corner to the line. Crease at the bottom.

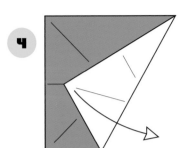

4

Unfold and rotate
model 180°.

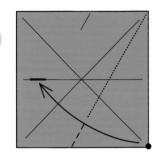

5

Repeat steps 3–4.

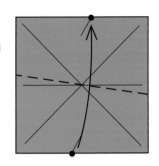

6

The dots will meet.

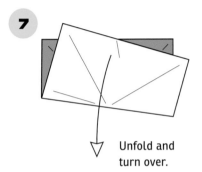

7

Unfold and
turn over.

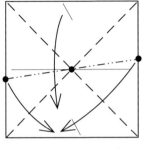

8

Push in at the center to collapse
along the creases. This is similar
to the waterbomb base.

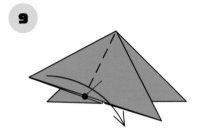

9

Fold down. Turn
over and repeat.

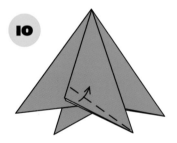

10

Fold the thin strip up
as high as possible.
Turn over and repeat.

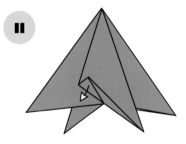

11

Unfold. Turn
over and repeat.

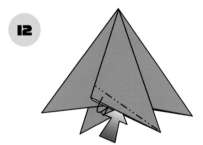

12

Sink by tucking between
the white layers. Turn
over and repeat.

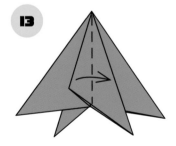

13

Fold to the right. Turn
over and repeat.

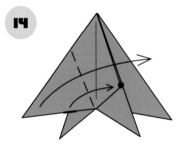

14

The edge will meet the
dot. Turn over and repeat.

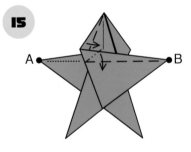

15

Imagine the line between A and
B. Squash-fold along that line.
Turn over and repeat.

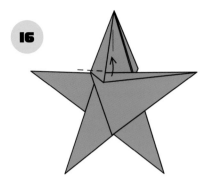

16

Fold up. Turn
over and repeat.

17

Sink. Turn over and repeat.

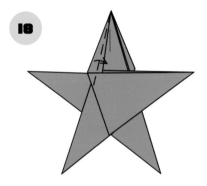

18

Fold a thin strip. Turn
over and repeat.

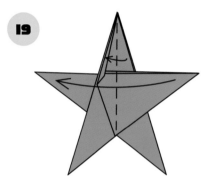

19

Fold two layers together.
Turn over and repeat.

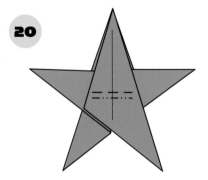

20

Lightly fold and unfold, without making
any crease, in both directions to keep
the model together.

21

Star

WONDER WOMAN'S ARROW

To become Wonder Woman, Diana endured numerous trials and contests. Even though her mother was the queen of Themyscira, the Amazonian princess had to compete against her sisters—all of them warriors from the day they were born. Hand-to-hand combat, sword fighting, marathon racing, and javelin throwing were among the tests. Diana also had to show prowess with the bow and arrow. As a young princess she delighted in developing her hand-eye coordination, perfect posture, and steady breath to loose arrows that always flew straight and true. Now Wonder Woman is a gifted athlete, a confident wielder of traditional weaponry, and an overpowering opponent in any showdown.

LEVEL: ★★☆

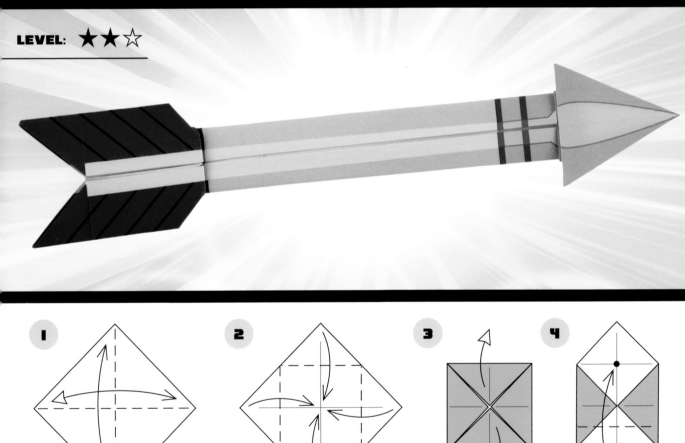

1 Fold and unfold.

2 Fold to the center.

3 Unfold.

4 Fold and unfold so the dots meet.

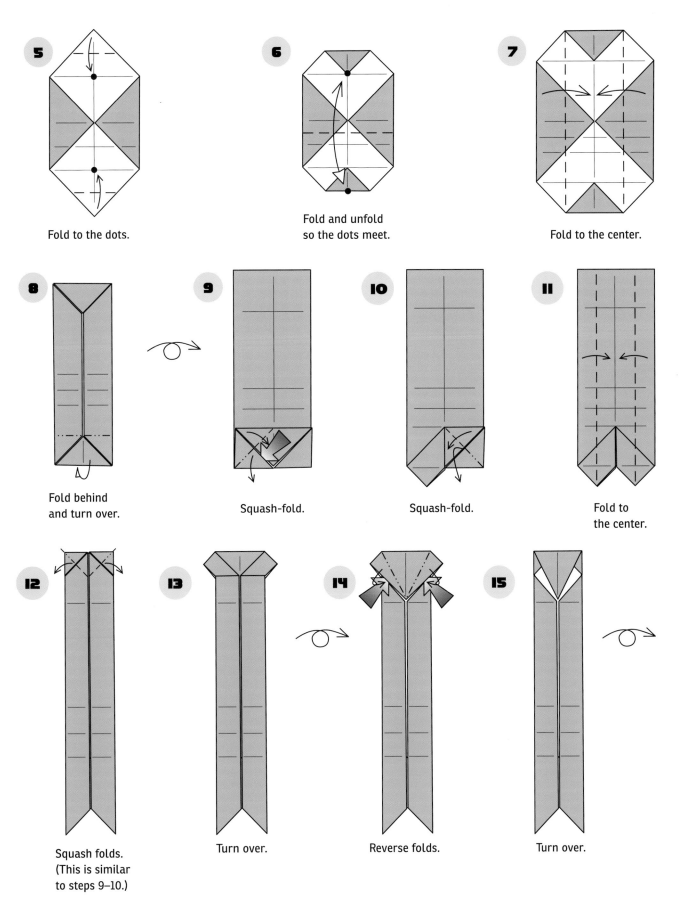

5 Fold to the dots.

6 Fold and unfold so the dots meet.

7 Fold to the center.

8 Fold behind and turn over.

9 Squash-fold.

10 Squash-fold.

11 Fold to the center.

12 Squash folds. (This is similar to steps 9–10.)

13 Turn over.

14 Reverse folds.

15 Turn over.

16

1. Fold down and swing out from behind.
2. Pleat-fold to the crease. Mountain-fold along the crease.

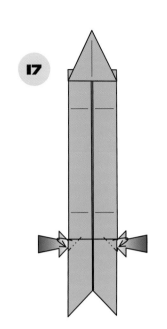

17

Reverse folds.

18

Turn over.

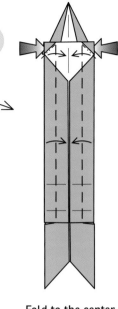

19

Fold to the center. Make small squash folds at the top.

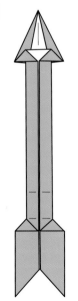

20

Turn over.

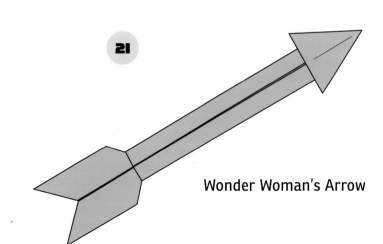

21

Wonder Woman's Arrow

WONDER WOMAN'S SWORD

Before she became Wonder Woman, Princess Diana had to prove she was worthy to be the first Amazon to enter the world of mortals. She competed against her sister-warriors to see who was the fastest, the strongest, and the best at wielding the weapons of war. Among her amazing arsenal was a magnificent sword. Forged by Vulcan, the weapons maker of the gods, Wonder Woman's sword is powerful enough to duel with other immortals, including Ares, the god of war. So mighty is her blade, the Amazonian princess only wields it in the gravest of situations.

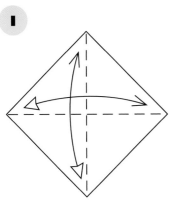

LEVEL: ★★☆

1

Fold and unfold.

2

Fold to the center.

3

Squash folds.

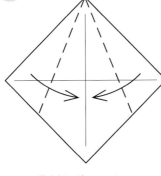

4

Fold down.

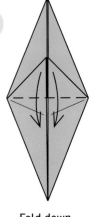

25

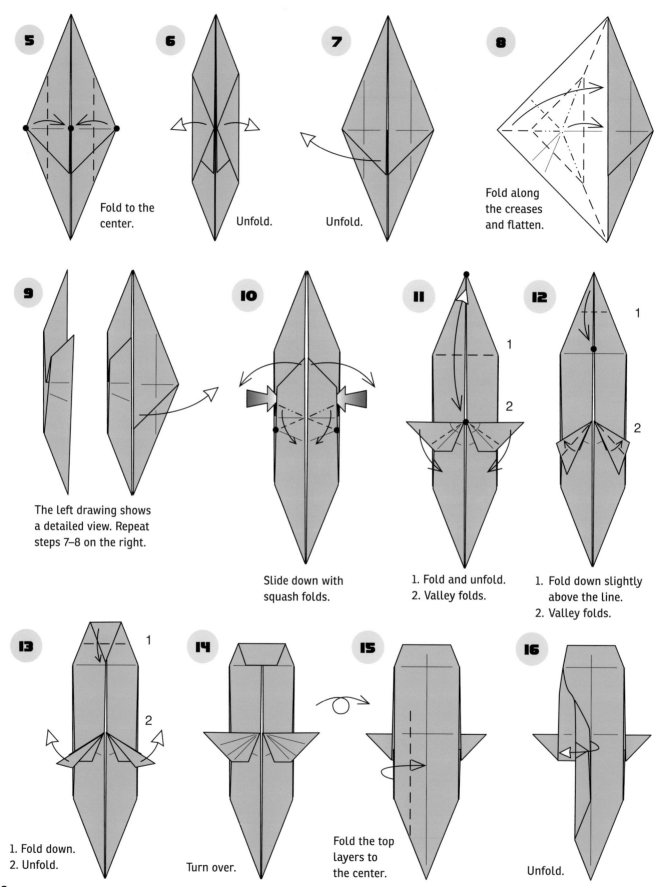

5 Fold to the center.

6 Unfold.

7 Unfold.

8 Fold along the creases and flatten.

9 The left drawing shows a detailed view. Repeat steps 7–8 on the right.

10 Slide down with squash folds.

11 1. Fold and unfold.
2. Valley folds.

12 1. Fold down slightly above the line.
2. Valley folds.

13 1. Fold down.
2. Unfold.

14 Turn over.

15 Fold the top layers to the center.

16 Unfold.

17 Repeat steps 15–16 on the right.

18 Pleat-fold.

19 Fold to the center with hidden squash folds.

20 Petal-fold.

21 Petal-fold.

22 Bend slightly down the center. Turn over.

23 Wonder Woman's Sword

EAGLE

When Wonder Woman first left her hidden home of Themyscira, she came to the United States eager to fight for liberty and justice among all humans. By adopting America as her second home, she also adopted the country's iconic colors and traditional symbols—including the eagle. Diana knew the eagle has symbolized royalty, authority, and power for dozens of countries, kingdoms, empires, and religions around the globe. For Wonder Woman, the radiant raptor makes a fitting emblem for a proud princess who strives to bring harmony to the entire planet.

LEVEL: ★★★

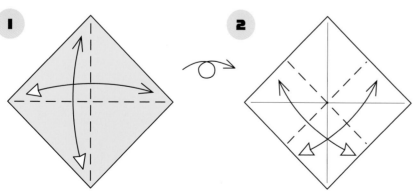

1

Fold and unfold.
Turn over.

2

Fold and unfold.

3

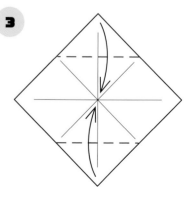

Fold to the center.

28

4

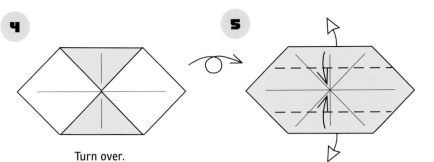

Turn over.

5

Fold to the center and
swing out from behind.

6

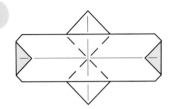

Fold in half.

7

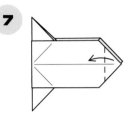

Fold the top layer to the
left. Repeat behind.

8

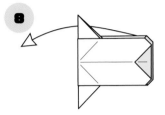

Unfold.

9

Fold and unfold
along the creases.

10

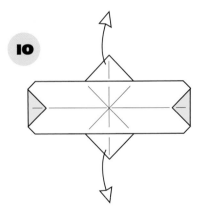

Unfold.

11

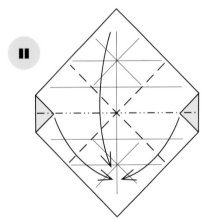

This is similar to the
preliminary fold.

12

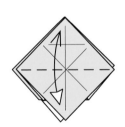

Fold and unfold the top
layer. Repeat behind.

13

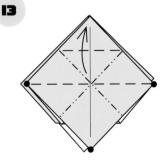

Fold along the creases.
The three dots will meet.
Repeat behind.

14

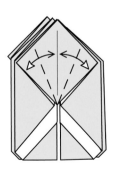

Fold and unfold.
Repeat behind.

15

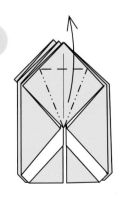

Petal-fold.
Repeat behind.

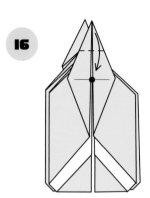
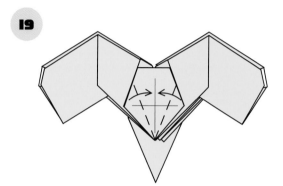

Fold the top flap
down to the dot.

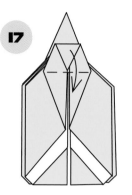

Fold down.

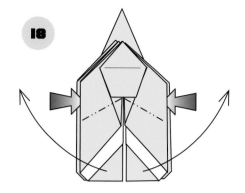

Reverse folds.
Rotate model 180°.

19
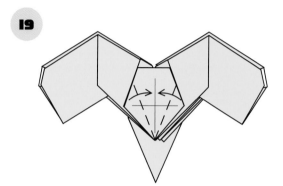

Fold to the center.

20
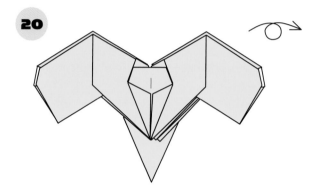

Turn over.

21
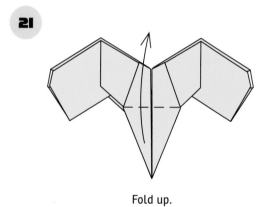

Fold up.

22
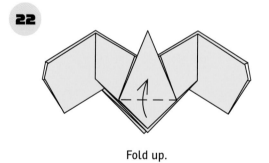

Fold up.

23
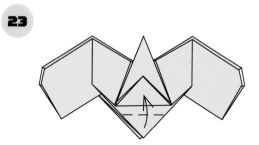

Fold up.

24

Fold behind.

30

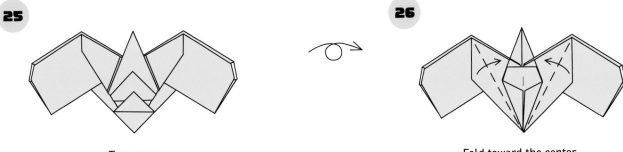

25

Turn over.

26

Fold toward the center.

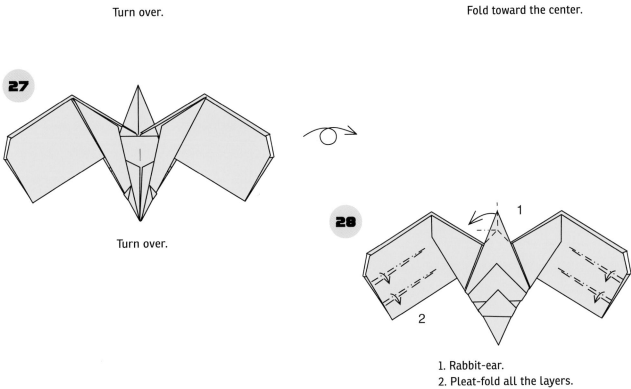

27

Turn over.

28

1. Rabbit-ear.
2. Pleat-fold all the layers.

29

Eagle

WONDER WOMAN SYMBOL

The iconic shape of the Princess of the Amazons' symbol perfectly suits its awe-inspiring hero. First and foremost, the golden double Ws stand for her alter ego as Wonder Woman. The solid interlocking letters also resemble bars of iron or steel, reminding evildoers of the hero's incredible strength and stamina. Finally, the design looks like a stylized eagle—Wonder Woman's alternate trademark—and has served as the chestplate of the champion's famous star-spangled uniform.

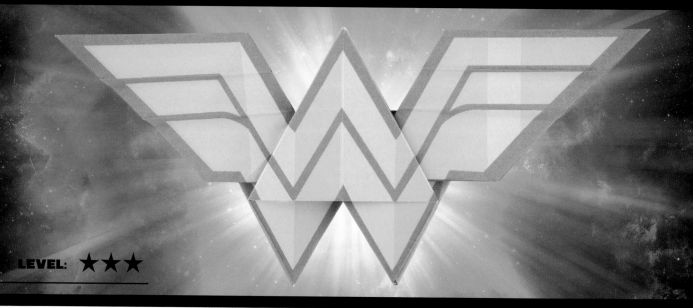

LEVEL: ★★★

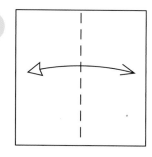

1

Fold and unfold.

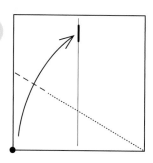

2

Bring the corner to the line. Crease on the left.

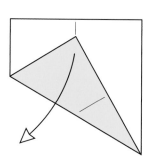

3

Unfold.

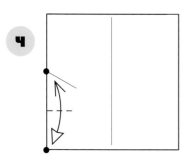

4

Fold and unfold on the left so the dots meet. Rotate model 180°.

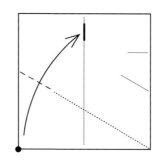

5

Repeat steps 2–4.

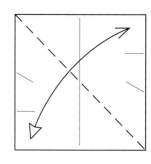

6

Fold and unfold. Rotate model.

7

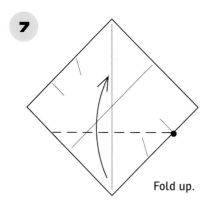

Fold up.

8

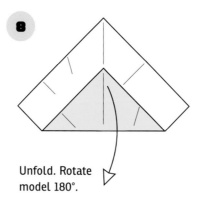

Unfold. Rotate model 180°.

9

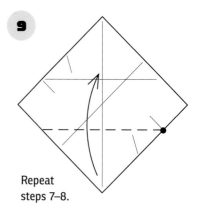

Repeat steps 7–8.

10

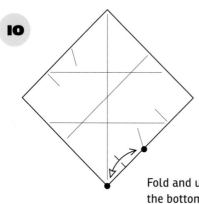

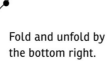

Fold and unfold by the bottom right.

11

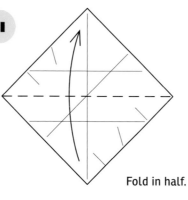

Fold in half.

12

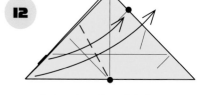

Bring the edge with the bold line to the upper dot.

13

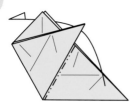

Fold behind along the edge of the top flap.

14

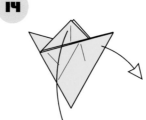

Unfold everything.

15

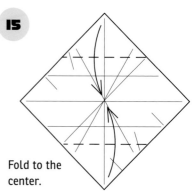

Fold to the center.

33

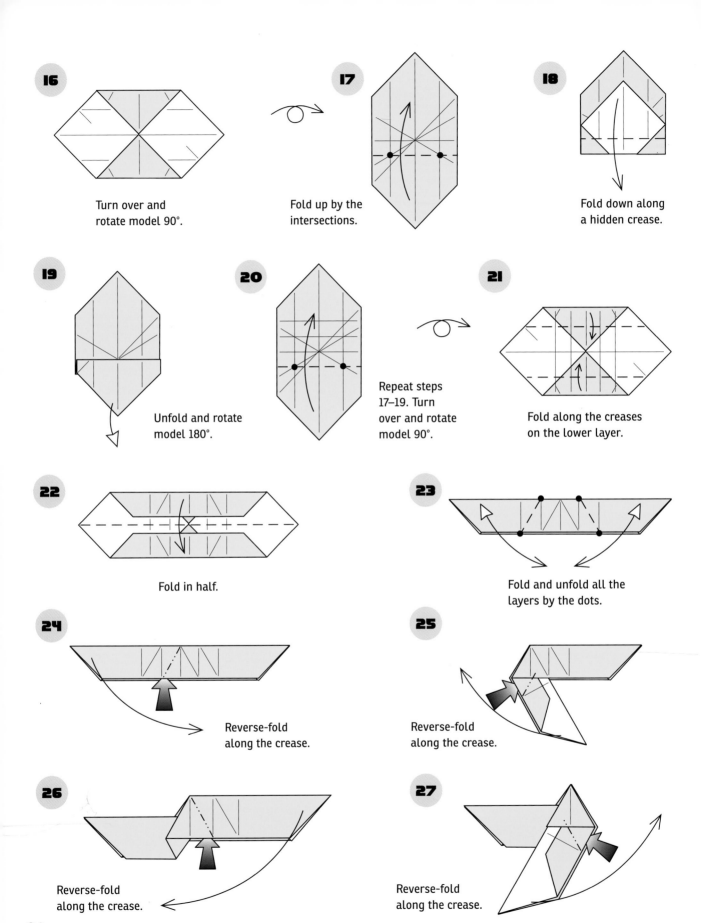

16 Turn over and rotate model 90°.

17 Fold up by the intersections.

18 Fold down along a hidden crease.

19 Unfold and rotate model 180°.

20 Repeat steps 17–19. Turn over and rotate model 90°.

21 Fold along the creases on the lower layer.

22 Fold in half.

23 Fold and unfold all the layers by the dots.

24 Reverse-fold along the crease.

25 Reverse-fold along the crease.

26 Reverse-fold along the crease.

27 Reverse-fold along the crease.

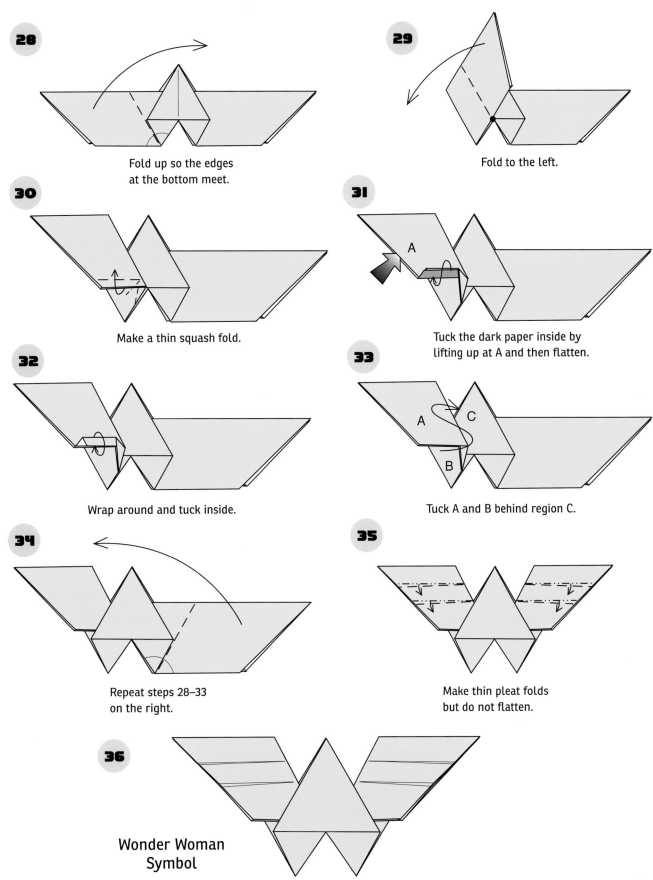

28 Fold up so the edges at the bottom meet.

29 Fold to the left.

30 Make a thin squash fold.

31 Tuck the dark paper inside by lifting up at A and then flatten.

32 Wrap around and tuck inside.

33 Tuck A and B behind region C.

34 Repeat steps 28–33 on the right.

35 Make thin pleat folds but do not flatten.

36 Wonder Woman Symbol

INVISIBLE JET

On the secret island of Themyscira, Wonder Woman learned to fly on air currents like a human paraglider. But when she needs speed, the Princess of the Amazons jumps into her supersonic turbojet. This high-tech aerodynamic aircraft was built by the immortal Amazonian engineers of Queen Hippolyta. Best of all, it's invisible! Villains never know the plane has invaded their airspace until Wonder Woman is already on the scene.

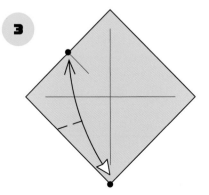

LEVEL: ★ ★ ★

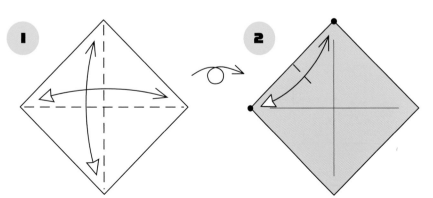

1
Fold and unfold.
Turn over.

2
Fold and unfold
on the edge.

3
Fold and unfold
on the edge.

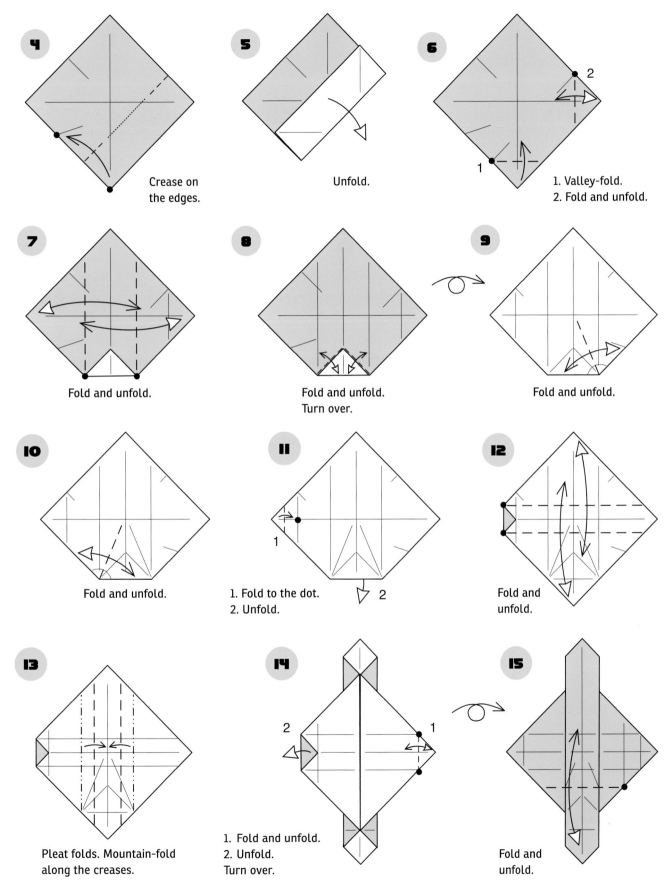

4
Crease on the edges.

5
Unfold.

6
2
1
1. Valley-fold.
2. Fold and unfold.

7
Fold and unfold.

8
Fold and unfold.
Turn over.

9
Fold and unfold.

10
Fold and unfold.

11
1
2
1. Fold to the dot.
2. Unfold.

12
Fold and unfold.

13
Pleat folds. Mountain-fold along the creases.

14
2
1
1. Fold and unfold.
2. Unfold.
Turn over.

15
Fold and unfold.

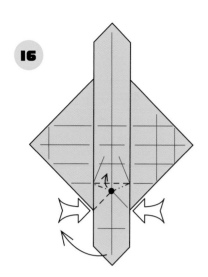

16

Lift up at the dot, push
in on the sides, and
fold along the creases.

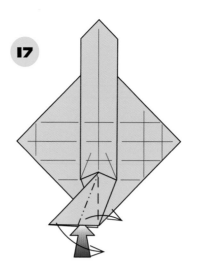

17

Squash-fold.

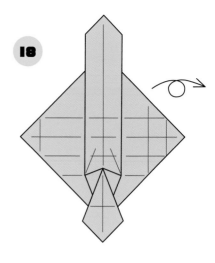

18

Turn over.

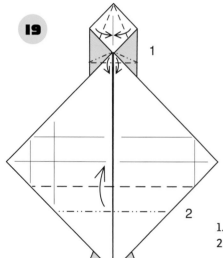

19

1. Squash folds.
2. Pleat-fold along
   the creases

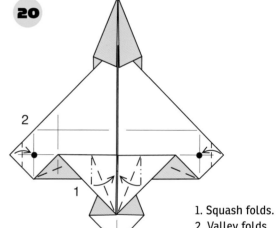

20

1. Squash folds.
2. Valley folds.

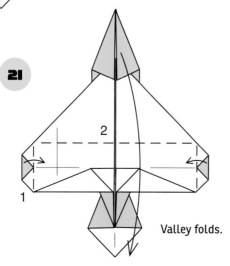

21

Valley folds.

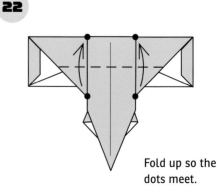

22

Fold up so the
dots meet.

38

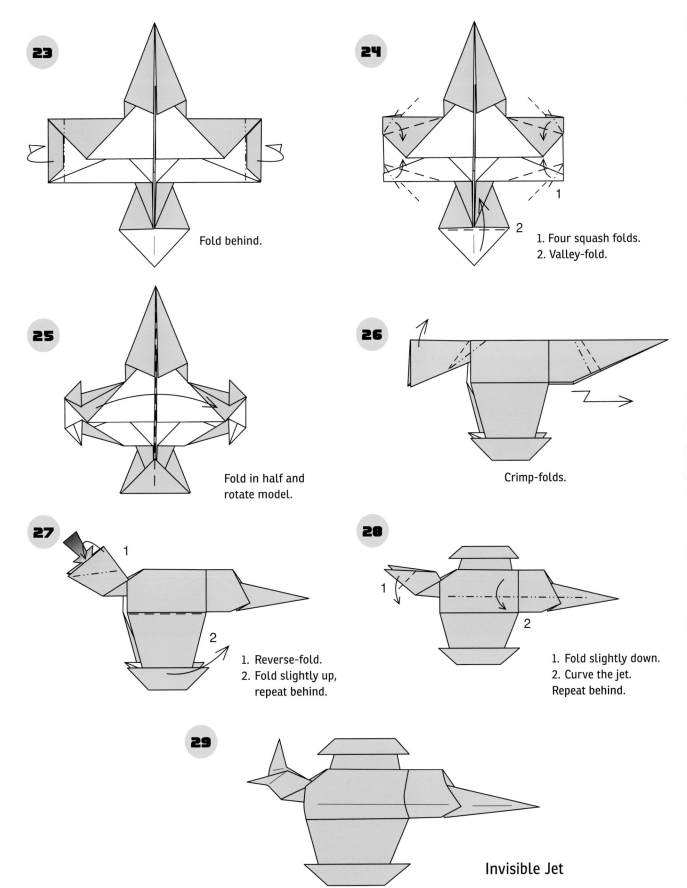

23 Fold behind.

24
1. Four squash folds.
2. Valley-fold.

25 Fold in half and rotate model.

26 Crimp-folds.

27
1. Reverse-fold.
2. Fold slightly up, repeat behind.

28
1. Fold slightly down.
2. Curve the jet. Repeat behind.

29 Invisible Jet

JUMPA THE KANGA

Kangas are found only on the secret island of Themyscira. Like kangaroos, they can leap long distances, but they're also lightning fast. These speedy steeds are the royal rides of the island's warrior race, the Amazons. Jumpa is Wonder Woman's loyal Super-Pet. This crime-kicking kanga carries royal weapons in her pouch, including a tiara, silver bracelets, and a Lasso of Truth.

LEVEL: ★★★

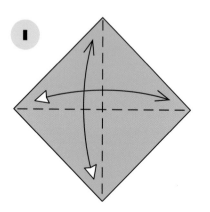

1

Fold and unfold.
Turn over.

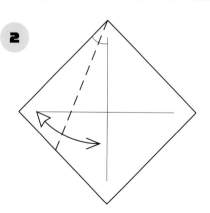

2

Fold and unfold.

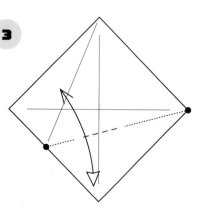

3

Fold and unfold
on the diagonal.

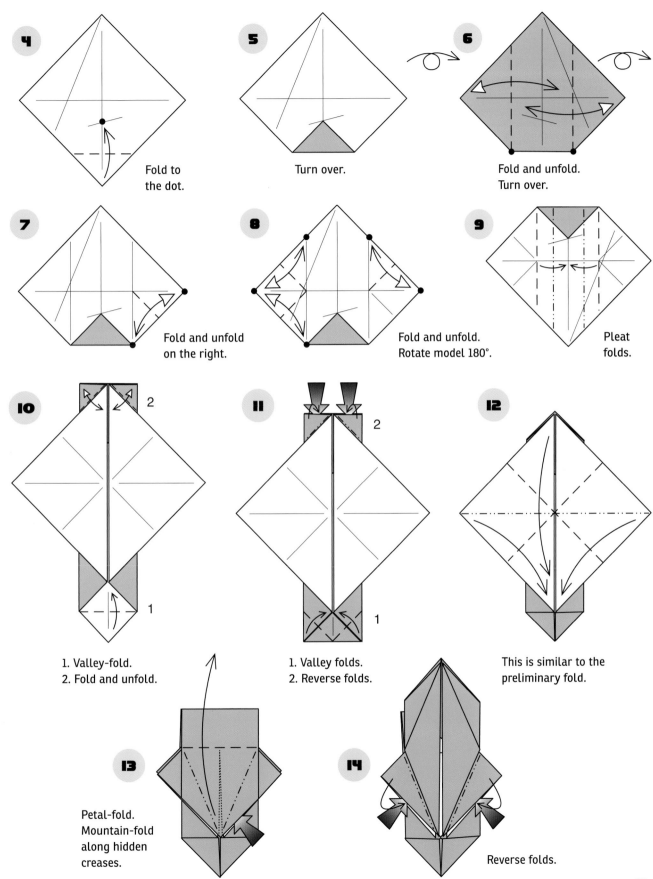

4 Fold to the dot.

5 Turn over.

6 Fold and unfold. Turn over.

7 Fold and unfold on the right.

8 Fold and unfold. Rotate model 180°.

9 Pleat folds.

10
1. Valley-fold.
2. Fold and unfold.

11
1. Valley folds.
2. Reverse folds.

12 This is similar to the preliminary fold.

13 Petal-fold. Mountain-fold along hidden creases.

14 Reverse folds.

15

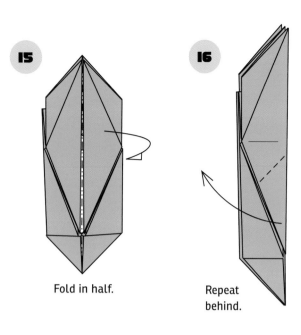

Fold in half.

16

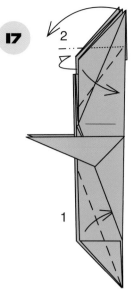

Repeat
behind.

17

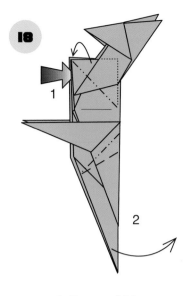

1. Tuck inside, repeat behind.
2. Crimp-fold.

18

1. Reverse-fold.
2. Crimp-fold.
Rotate model.

19

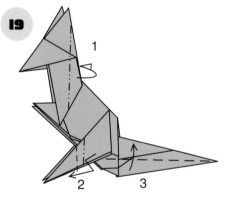

1. Fold behind.
2. Crimp-fold.
3. Valley-fold.
Repeat behind.

20

1. Shape the ear.
2. Reverse-fold.
3. Fold inside.
4. Curl the tail.
5. Shape the back.
Repeat behind.

21

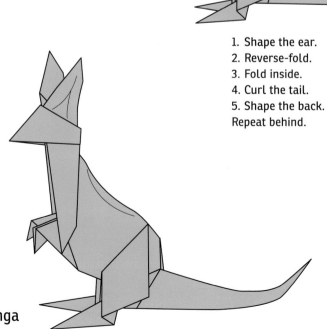

Jumpa the Kanga

42

WONDER WOMAN

A world at war. Countries in chaos. Humanity without harmony. The planet cried out for a hero, but would that cry be heard? In Earth's darkest hour, the Amazons on the secret island of Themyscira held a trial to find their strongest and bravest champion. From that contest one warrior triumphed over all: Wonder Woman. With an Invisible Jet and invincible weapons, the Princess of the Amazons boldly entered the world of mortals. Her mission to bring peace, defend justice, and restore harmony across the globe has only just begun.

LEVEL: ★★★

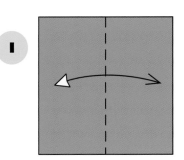

1

Fold and unfold.
Turn over.

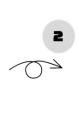

2

Fold and unfold.

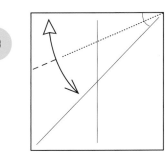

3

Fold to the crease and unfold. Crease on the left.

4

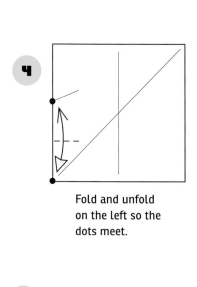

Fold and unfold on the left so the dots meet.

5

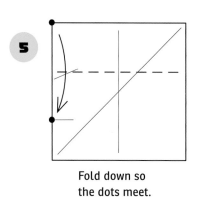

Fold down so the dots meet.

6

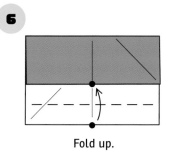

Fold up.

7

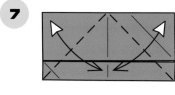

Fold and unfold.

8

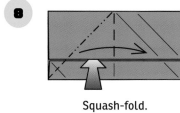

Squash-fold.

9

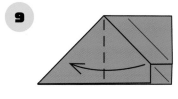

Fold the top flap.

10

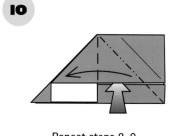

Repeat steps 8–9 on the right.

11

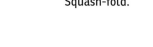

Turn over.

12

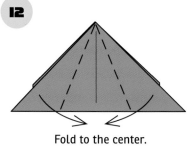

Fold to the center.

13

Unfold.

14

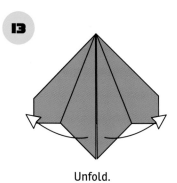

Reverse folds.

15

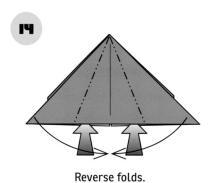

Fold and unfold the top flaps to the center.

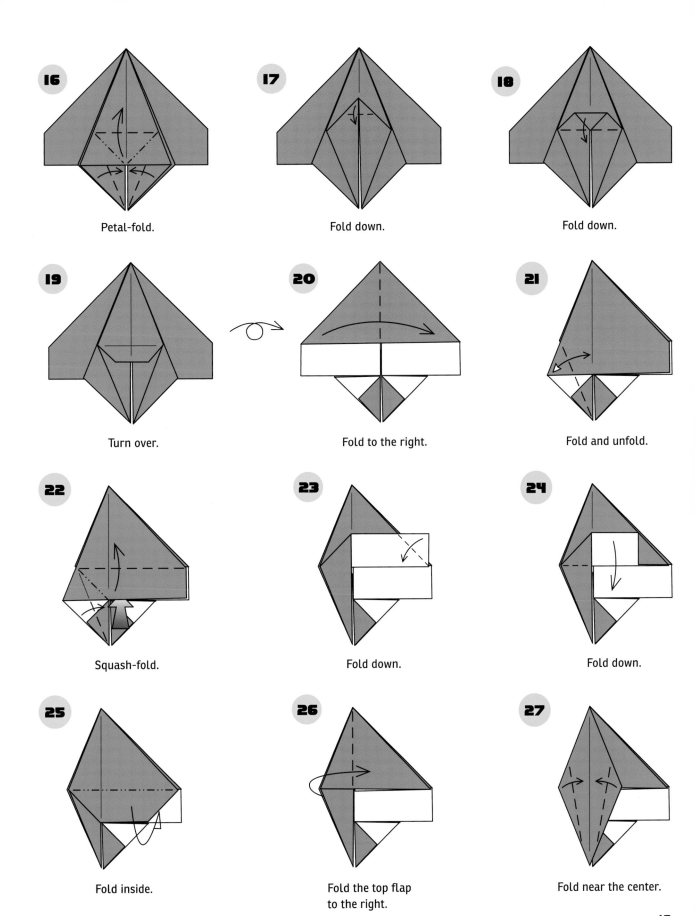

16 Petal-fold.

17 Fold down.

18 Fold down.

19 Turn over.

20 Fold to the right.

21 Fold and unfold.

22 Squash-fold.

23 Fold down.

24 Fold down.

25 Fold inside.

26 Fold the top flap to the right.

27 Fold near the center.

28

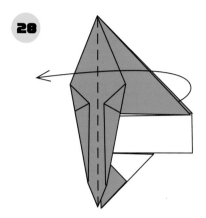

Fold to the left.

29

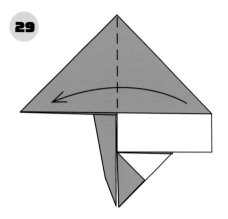

Repeat steps 20–28 in
the opposite direction.

30

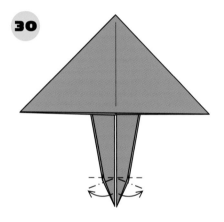

Squash folds.

31

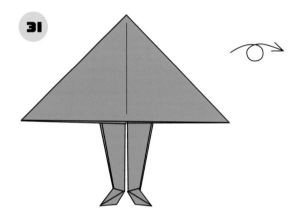

Turn over.

32

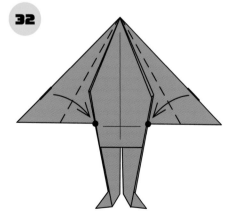

Bring the edges
to the dots.

33

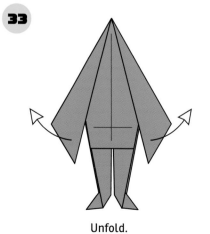

Unfold.

34

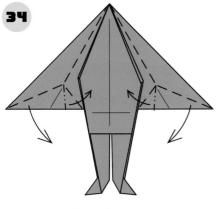

Shape the arms
with rabbit ears.

35

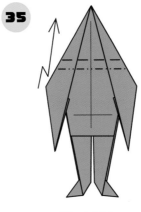

Pleat-fold.

36

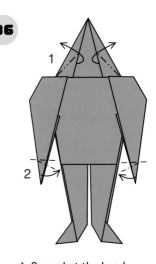

1. Spread at the head.
2. Squash-fold the hands.

37

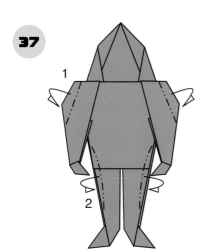

1. Fold behind.
2. Shape the body and legs.

38

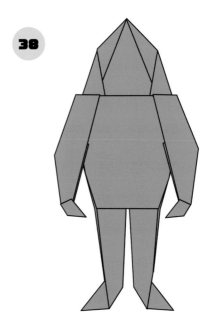

Wonder Woman

READ MORE

Harbo, Christopher. *Origami Papertainment: Samurai, Owls, Ninja Stars, and More!* Origami Paperpalooza. North Mankato, Minn.: Capstone Press, 2015.

Montroll, John. *Origami Stars.* Mineola, N.Y.: Dover Publications, 2014.

Montroll, John. *Superman Origami: Amazing Folding Projects Featuring the Man of Steel.* DC Origami. North Mankato, Minn.: Capstone Press, 2015.

Robinson, Nick. *The Awesome Origami Pack.* Hauppauge, N.Y.: Barron's, 2014.

INTERNET SITES

FactHound offers a safe, fun way to find Internet sites related to this book. All of the sites on FactHound have been researched by our staff.

Here's all you do:

Visit *www.facthound.com*

Type in this code: 9781491417881

Super-cool stuff! Check out projects, games and lots more at www.capstonekids.com

ABOUT THE AUTHOR

John Montroll is respected for his work in origami throughout the world. His published work has significantly increased the global repertoire of original designs in origami. John is also acknowledged for developing new techniques and groundbreaking bases. The American origami master is known for being the inspiration behind the single-square, no cuts, no glue approach in origami.

John started folding in elementary school. He quickly progressed from folding models from books to creating his own designs. John has written many books, and each model that he designs has a meticulously developed folding sequence. John's long-standing experience allows him to accomplish a model in fewer steps rather than more. It is his constant endeavor to give the reader a pleasing folding experience.

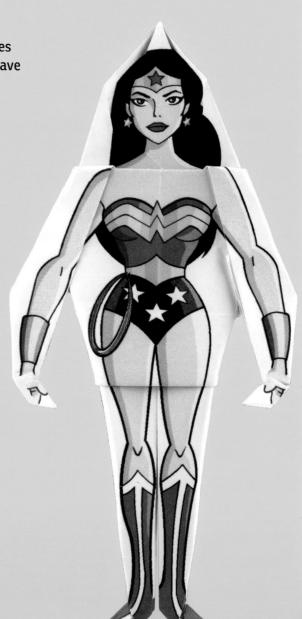